AF413111

Does Alcoholism Have a Big Silver Lining?

Does the Alcoholic Hit Rock Bottom Earlier Than Others Do?

Loran Joly

Copyright © 2024 by Loran Joly

All rights reserved.

To all of those who find it hard to keep hope...

Chapter 1

Is Alcoholism a Gift?

I s Alcoholism a Gift, in a sense?

For is it one of the few ways of running from our fears, anger and guilt, that has a special set of silver linings?

I wish to explore this.

For some have said, No Pain, No Gain; and others talk of The Gift of Pain...

So, are Alcoholics The Lucky Ones, perhaps, in that they are perhaps some of the Few who are forced to face up to their Running, *before* their deathbed?

Or before the Wakeup Call of a massive heart attack, cancer, or loss of a child, or very injurious crime?

Chapter 2

What Causes a Rock Bottom Experience?

Now, what causes this massive Pain, in the Alcoholic? And why, in general, is it said they have eventually "hit rock bottom" and are then forced to face up to Reality?

Or put another way, why are non-alcoholics, with their own non-chemical "drugs of choice", *not* hitting rock bottom?

Chapter 3

Don't We Either Run From or Face Our Fears?

First of all, I believe that we all prefer to do not only what is easiest in life, hence the "short-term" mentality, but secondly, too, we want guarantees on anything that is going to take a big investment: in time or a series of pains to be faced.

So, we have heard of the idea of "short-term" expediency-seeking.

But yet, we don't always pursue the short-term, do we?

We may sign up for a schooling program that takes years, say.

Why?

Because we have an idea that the payoff of a long-term venture in certain areas, will have a significant likelihood of paying off.

Whereas other pursuits are a real gamble, such as going to

Hollywood, or film school to become a Director, or entering psychoanalysis, say.

And so, given the options of either running, or facing our fears, we likely would Run, Run, Run, rather than take the more questionable path of facing our fears for a period of years - or as long as it takes to break through most all of them

* * *

.

Yes, we have no sense of whether facing our fears and anger and guilt will in fact have any more guarantee of success, after five or ten years, say, then going to Hollywood, hoping to be the next Star.

Or put it this way:

If someone said that if you used nail-clippers instead of a lawnmower, to cut your lawn, for the next five years, you would develop such patience and have so many insights, that you would become a Star at something?

Well, most would not want to take the risk of doing all that effort - all of that suffering, if you will - without a considerable guarantee of a successful payoff.

So, most all of us do the SENSIBLE thing - the thing with a far more likely payoff - Running.

. . .

In some fashion.

Chapter 4

Why Doesn't The Alcoholic Switch to Some Other Way of Coping?

So, perhaps the biggie question, is this: why do some people use Alcohol to cope with fears, anger and their conscience - guilt, in other words - while others have their favorite *"non-chemical"* "bottles-of-choice?"

Why can't the Alcoholic SWITCH to a <u>NON</u>-CHEMICAL form of running, thus?

And thus, is said to have Relapses, all too often, and a so-called genetic predisposition to using alcohol, too?

Hence, the phrase, at exiting a rehab, sometimes, of "See you back in thirty days"?

Chapter 5

We All Have "Relapses"

Well, I would speculatively say that we all have "RELAPSES" - to using our preferred defense mechanisms, call these our favorite "bottles", when under immense stress, or triggered by something.

We thus "relapse" to more "coping" than average, here and there.

Exactly like, when tired, we might say we "relapse" into sleeping for the night, or taking a nap, at least.

Only, *these* relapses don't cause job losses, financial pains, or a prison term, nearly as often.

And so are not called "relapses," but simply "overindulgences".

Indeed, under periods of high stress, we might well find our bodies "relapsing" into a cold or pneumonia or bronchitis....

Yes, we are temporarily infected with lots of stress-manifestations"....

Chapter 6

Alcoholics as Nice People?

So, if the use of too much alcohol as a "coping mechanism" is so injurious to survival, then why doesn't the Alcoholic simply SWITCH to something LESS injurious? Why do they "insist" upon repeatedly using Alcohol, and not switch to some other "bottle-of-choice" of a non-chemical nature?

Well, I would speculate further, that this may tie in to how the person who struggles with being despondent at times - feeling hopeless - aka "depressed," some say, generally are very *"nice"* people.

Empathetic.

And I then tie the alcoholic into this same group, of "nice" people - of empathetic people, basically speaking.

Even though it is said that the alcoholic is subject to periods of rage, and perhaps hitting someone, at times.

But does this expressed rage and more, reflect a lack of empathy, or is there a different source?

Does the rage and more, come from an inability to keep a job, followed by loss of living quarters?

Or perhaps some prison time?

Not a lack of empathy?

* * *

The alcoholic may well be what I call "empathetically-constrained" to not turn to other defense mechanisms, or "bottles-of-choice" that do not involve self-harm, basically speaking.

They are not thus likely to be a "status"-"bottle" user, or user of over-control. Or use isolating, either.

They LIKE people, and that is the "problem"!

So, they cannot turn to "substances" other than alcohol without violating their orientation toward empathy.

They won't seek to "get over" on people thus.

And so, if they won't do things that regularly end up harming others, because this violates their empathetic orientation, then what else is there to do, other than to use "copers" that are not harming others, even if harmful to themselves?

This is perhaps a speculative statement....

and why won't the alcoholic switch then to some other drugs of choices I would call it to include being over controlling, or using status in the sense of elevation of what thoughts about themselves and putting others down? hence why won't they use the pleasures of making others feel worse about themselves in order to cope with their own problems of fear and anger?

Put another way, they refuse to do what might make themselves feel better, if someone else will be injured.

They'd thus rather starve to death than "rob" someone else - and by someone, I mean a lot of people, over time.

Chapter 7

What is Rock-Bottoming?

So, the alcoholic is often said to "hit rock bottom", if legal or monetary forces "take" the alcohol from them, and they have nowhere else to turn without a lot of others being hurt.

Whereas others do not have to stick to this empathy-orientation, and are much freer to use "copers" which do not as easily cause job loss, financial calamity or prison time.

Putting others down, say, as a way of coping, will not land someone in prison or cause financial calamity, likely....

Chapter 8

The Rock Bottom of the Alcoholic Happens Much Earlier Than a Heart Attack Rock Bottom...

hy, thus, might over-use of alcohol be a gift, a pain with a silver lining?

Well, a physician has said, that his cancer patients tell him that cancer was the best thing that ever happened to them.

It was a "wakeup call".

Or thus, it took cancer or some other calamity to make them face a key Reality in life that they were running from, for decades.

Yet the running had not caused job losses or a financial melt-down, or prison time, even.

Cancer - or thus, their Deathbed - ends up being their Rock Bottom time - when nothing but Facing Reality will do any good.

For, status or some new vacation-of-choice, or new "boat," will mean absolutely nothing, when one has cancer, say. In this case, their orientation on empathy doesn't constrain them not to turn to other "copers".

It's just that all such coping mechanisms or "bottles" no longer have any potency.

Hence, alcohol may be a Gift, because it "strikes" earlier than cancer as a Buck Stops Here moment, and one then has more time left in life, to reap the happinesses of a life of change.

Chapter 9

Other Rock Bottoms as Silver Linings

Simply put then, the Lucky Ones are those, who have their Rock Bottom moment earlier rather than later, in life.

This too could be applied to the lives of those who lose a child; or have a massive heart attack; or lose a leg, say, or lose their vision.

All these are surely so halting to life's happinesses, that we could call these "rock bottom" events, too - or Gifts of Bottom-Pain.

About the Author

The author welcomes contact at message@goldpogo.com
He spent many years helping an "alcoholic" achieve freedom.

www.ingramcontent.com/pod-product-compliance
Lightning Source LLC
Chambersburg PA
CBHW040038150726
48196CB00045B/934